THE RISE OF MAMMALS

"THE RISE OF

MAMMALS "

ROY A. GALLANT

ILLUSTRATIONS BY
ANNE CANEVARI GREEN

A FIRST BOOK
FRANKLIN WATTS 1986
NEW YORK • LONDON
TORONTO • SYDNEY

FRONTIS: A SABER-TOOTHED TIGER
TRIES TO GUARD ITS KILL FROM VULTURES
IN CALIFORNIA'S LA BREA TAR PITS.

Photographs courtesy of: Department of Library Services, American
Museum of Natural History: pp. 2 (#328188), 17 (#313953), 18 (#328192),
21 (#38529, K.C. Lenskjold), 33 (#35775, H.S. Rice), 35 (top-#45559,
E.O. Hovey), 37 (#35777, H.S. Rice), 43 (#35837), 49 (#37952,
Julius Kirschner), 54 (top-#311813, Julius Kirschner), 54 (bottom-
#311665, Julius Kirschner), 57 (#320660, T.L. Bierwert), 65 (#120708),
69 (#322602), 70 (#323739, Rota), 84 (#323617); Field Museum of
Natural History, painting by Charles R. Knight: pp. 20, 34, 35 (bottom);
U.S. Department of the Interior, Geological Survey: pp. 25, 66;
Chicago Natural History Museum: p. 30; Field Museum of Natural
History, painting by John Conrad Hansen: p. 40; UPI/Bettmann
Newsphotos: pp. 59, 60, 76; The Bettmann Archive: p. 73.

Library of Congress Cataloging in Publication Data

Gallant, Roy A.
The rise of mammals.

(A First book)
Includes index.
Summary: Traces the development of mammal species,
including human beings, during the Cenozoic era.
1. Mammals, Fossil—Juvenile literature.
(1. Mammals, Fossil) I. Green, Anne Canevari, ill.
II. Title. III. Series.
QE881.G24 1986   569   86-11161
ISBN 0-531-10206-8

CONTENTS

FOR TEEJAY

ACKNOWLEDGMENTS

My thanks to Dr. George Kukla
of the Lamont Doherty
Geological Observatory,
Palisades, New Jersey, for
his thoroughness in reviewing
the manuscript of this book
for accuracy.

THE RISE OF MAMMALS

CHAPTER ONE

MAJOR EVENTS
IN THE
AGE OF MAMMALS

The Age of Mammals began about 65 million years ago. Geologists call this period of time the Cenozoic era. The name comes from the Greek words *kainos*, meaning "recent," and *zoe*, meaning "life." So this geologic time span is the era of recent life on Earth.

THE TERTIARY PERIOD

The Cenozoic era is divided into two periods. The first of these is called the Tertiary period, meaning "third." The Tertiary spanned 63 million years; it began 65 million years ago and ended 1.8 million years ago.

By about halfway through this period Earth's continents had moved about and taken up the positions where we now find them. Earlier, geologists tell us, all of Earth's landmasses had been clumped together as the supercontinent called Pangaea. Then, about 220 million years ago, Pangaea broke into two smaller continents, a northern half (Laurasia) and a southern half (Gondwana). It was during the Tertiary that Laurasia and Gondwana broke apart into smaller landmasses, which drifted to the positions of the continents we know today.

THE EARTH IN TIME
Numbers = millions of years ago

MESOZOIC ERA
"Age of Reptiles"

PALEOZOIC ERA
"Ancient Life"

190 M. YEARS AGO

215
PERMIAN | TRIASSIC | JURASSIC | CRETACEOUS
155 | 120
70 MILLION YEARS AGO

530 | CAMBRIAN
440

235 | MISSISSIPPIAN
PENNSYL-VANIAN ("Age of Amphibians")
265 | DEVONIAN | SILURIAN | ORDO-VICIAN
("Age of Fishes")
330 | 365

PRECAMBRIAN ERA

CENOZOIC ERA
"Recent Life"

PROTEROZOIC

TERTIARY

1.8

QUA-TERNARY

ARCHAEOZOIC

4.5 billion years ago

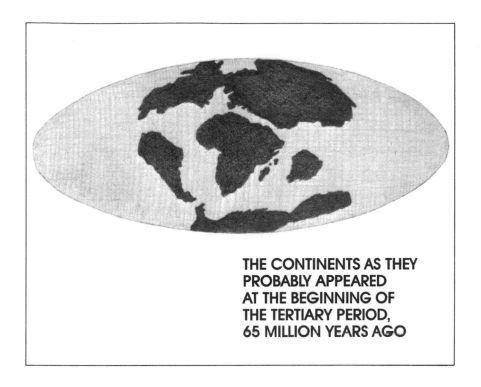

THE CONTINENTS AS THEY PROBABLY APPEARED AT THE BEGINNING OF THE TERTIARY PERIOD, 65 MILLION YEARS AGO

By about the beginning of the Tertiary, many reptiles of earlier times, including the dinosaurs, had died out. That earlier era, which had lasted some 180 million years, had been known as the Age of Reptiles. The great period of dying out of the giant reptiles, who had ruled the land for more than 100 million years, ushered in the Age of Mammals. The first mammals had lived during the time the reptiles were king, but they were small, ratlike animals. Not until later did they evolve into the many different kinds of mammals we know today.

Some of those mammals of Tertiary times took up life in the sea (whales and seals, for example). Others took to the

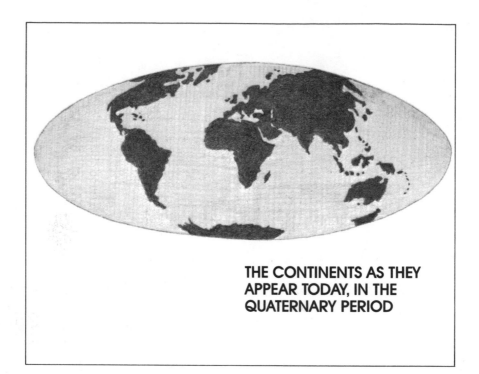

**THE CONTINENTS AS THEY
APPEAR TODAY, IN THE
QUATERNARY PERIOD**

air (bats, for instance). Among the land mammals that roamed the planet at the close of the Tertiary were some giants—the mastodons, some 18-foot-high (5-m) ground sloths, giant bison, and 7-foot-long (2-m) beavers.

By the middle to late Tertiary period nearly all of the main types of birds known to us today were common. Cats, wolves, and dogs had also evolved by this time. Most of the inland seas, which earlier had covered large parts of the continents, dried up during this period. And, as the climate gradually cooled, grasslands began to spread.

During the Tertiary there was widespread volcanic activity in the western United States, where Mounts Shasta and

Many giant mammals, such as the 7-foot-long (2.1-m) beavers depicted here, roamed the planet at the close of the Tertiary.

By the beginning of the Quaternary, horses had appeared.
These shown here are known as Mesohippus biardi.

Rainier were formed. The great Alpine and Himalayan mountain ranges were built, and a good part of the Andes and Rockies were thrust up. There was also volcanic activity in the northwestern United States, in the North Atlantic region, in East Africa, and in the Mediterranean region. Meanwhile, huge glaciers formed in Antarctica.

THE QUATERNARY PERIOD

The second of the two periods of the Cenozoic era is called the Quaternary period, meaning "fourth." It began 1.8 million years ago and is the geologic period we live in today.

By the beginning of the Quaternary, horses had evolved. Of the several humanlike branches that evolved, only our own type (*Homo sapiens*) survived. Ice sheets blanketed the continents of North America and northern Europe, while glaciers filled the valleys in high mountain regions. The mountains of the west coast of North America have also been active geologically throughout Quaternary times, with widespread volcanoes that continue to erupt to this day.

There have been many advances and retreats of glaciers in the Quaternary. Fossils from many parts of North America are evidence that many large beasts roamed the land during parts of the last ice age. But most of them became extinct after the ice began to melt. There were giant bison, giant beavers, giant ground sloths, cave bears, giant armadillos, woolly mammoths, mastodons, woolly rhinoceroses, and saber-toothed cats.

Why so many giant animals? According to biologists, a cold climate favors large animals, since large animals lose body heat at a slower rate than do smaller animals. Some of the ice-age animals, such as ground sloths and giant armadillos, came northward into the southern United States from South America. Others, such as horses, saber-toothed cats,

During parts of the last ice age, many large
beasts, including the giant ground sloths and
royal bison shown here, roamed the land.

mammoths, antelopes, and musk-oxen, crossed over a bridge of land then linking Alaska with Asia.

By 8,000 years ago, North America's elephants, camels, horses, dire wolves, and longhorn bison were all gone. The mammals we know today are but a handful of leftovers that survived from earlier times. The levels of the Quaternary seas have varied with the buildup and melting of glacial ice. As the ice melts, more water is added to the oceans; then the coming of a new ice age removes water from the oceans and locks it up as ice for thousands of years.

With that general view of the Age of Mammals, we will now look more closely at some of the major animals that have evolved over the past 2 million years, including humans.

CHAPTER TWO

LIFE DURING
THE TERTIARY
PERIOD

CHANGES ON THE LAND

As the continents continued to move apart during the Mesozoic era and Tertiary period, a great crack in Earth's crust
formed between North America and Europe and between
South America and Africa. The crack became known as the
Mid-Atlantic Ridge. As it kept growing wider, Europe and Africa on one side and North and South America on the oppo-
site side drifted apart. This produced a widening Atlantic
Ocean, and the process continues to this day. Alaska
became connected to and disconnected from Asia several
times during the Tertiary.

In the Southern Hemisphere, South America broke its link
with Antarctica, as that great southern continent took up its
present position at the South Pole. Due to the harsh new climate, Antarctica lost most of its life forms. Antarctica also
broke its link with Australia early in the Tertiary, or right before;
this permitted Australia to drift northward into a warmer climate.

The east coast of the United States during the Tertiary
was not very active geologically. Erosion wore down and
rounded the Appalachian Mountains, and in the process

washed large amounts of sediments into the Atlantic from Cape Cod in the north all the way down to Florida and into the eastern Gulf of Mexico.

The situation was different in the west. When the Tertiary began, the Pacific Ocean washed its way inland as far as the present position of the foothills of the Sierra Nevada Range. Massive outpourings of lava covered vast areas of Oregon and Washington states. Geologists have counted 23 separate lava flows on the Columbia Plateau. There were many volcanic outbursts that buried vast areas of the western United States beneath layers of ash. The Yellowstone Park area of Wyoming and the San Juan Mountains of Colorado were especially hard hit. The Coast Ranges were thrust up, and the Rocky Mountains continued to push higher from earlier times. Over a period of 20 million years the Rockies were raised several thousand feet. Also raised higher were the Black Hills of South Dakota and the Teton Range of Wyoming.

About 25 million years ago the famous San Andreas Fault seems to have been formed. This is a great crack in the rock crust running north and south a few miles inland along most of California's coast. From time to time, movements of crustal rock cause the two faces of the fault to rub against each other and snap, producing earthquakes.

Coal deposits laid down during the Tertiary have been found in Alaska. Fossils of vertebrates (animals with backbones) seem to be missing here, but they are plentiful farther south. Sediments deposited about midway through the Tertiary in the foothills and plains regions of South Dakota,

The San Andreas Fault, a great crack in Earth's rock crust, was formed in the Tertiary period.

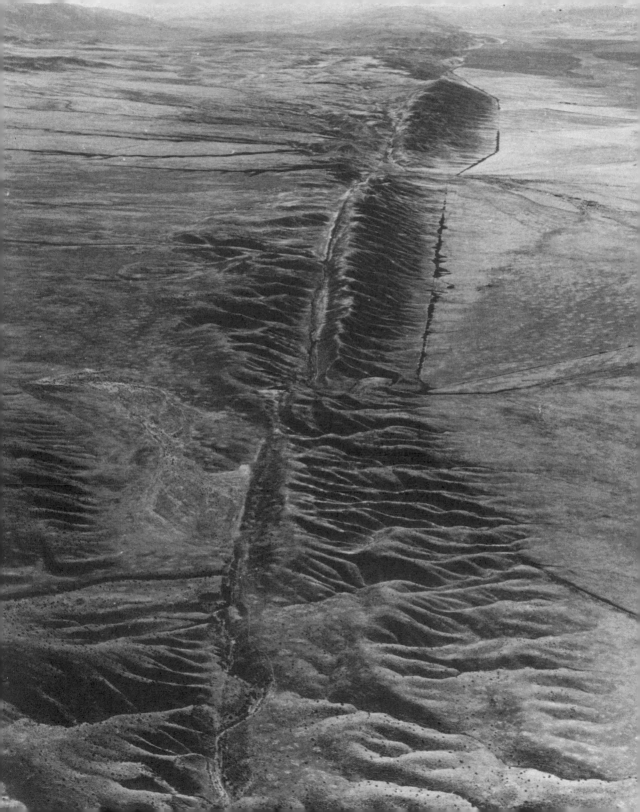

Nebraska, Wyoming, and Colorado contain the best-preserved fossils of mammals found anywhere in the world today. During the last years of the Tertiary widespread sediments rich with fossil plants and animals of the time were again laid down over areas of the western plains. And again, the source of those sediments was the Rocky Mountain range.

The end of the Tertiary was marked by a continuing trend of cooling and drying. Mammals that had evolved earlier and that had adapted to a warm, moist climate could not survive the new climate and became extinct. Other mammals took their place. The climate of the late Tertiary set the stage for the great ice age that was to grip the Quaternary period.

The most dramatic geological changes during the Tertiary began early in the period, about 53 million years ago. At that time the African continent moved slowly northward and collided with Europe. The massive African giant continued ramming Europe throughout the Tertiary. The collision pushed up the Alps in Europe, the Himalayan Mountains of Asia, the Pyrenees of France, and the Atlas Mountains of northwest Africa.

CHANGES IN
PLANTS AND ANIMALS

The Tertiary was a challenging time for plants and animals alike. Many changes of climate during the period brought extremes in heat and cold, times of abundant rain and snow, and long periods of drought.

In spite of these environmental challenges, no other geologic period saw so many different kinds of organisms adapting to so many severe environmental conditions. Plants and animals alike took up life deep in the oceans, in caves, in the many new mountain ranges, in deserts, in the ice-free regions of the poles, and many other places (or habitats). When the English naturalist Charles Darwin visited South America in the 1830s he was amazed at the many kinds of living organisms he found. He wrote: "We may well affirm that every part of the world is habitable! Whether lakes of brine, or those underground ones hidden beneath volcanic mountains, or warm mineral springs, or the wide expanse and depths of the ocean, or the upper regions of the atmosphere, and even the surface of perpetual snow—all support living things."

Most of the plants familiar to us today evolved during Tertiary times. We have found fossil remains of many kinds of mosses, bacteria, fungi, molds, and flowering plants. Gone, or about to lose their importance, were the giant horsetails, fern trees, and cycads that for so long had ruled the land. Replacing them were the trees we know today—pines, firs, and cedars, for example.

Especially successful were the flowering plants that had become established earlier in the Cretaceous. Among the most successful of these were many kinds of grasses, of which there are now more than 5,000 different types, including crop plants such as wheat, corn, rice, oats, barley, sugarcane, and millet. The widespread grasses, and the seeds they produced, meant a plentiful food supply for the many grazing animals and birds that evolved during the Tertiary.

Life in the Tertiary oceans seems to have been less lively than in the warmer waters of the Cretaceous. The cephalopods, mollusks who lived in long, cone-shaped shells, had almost disappeared by the end of the Tertiary. But for some reason their relatives without shells, including octopuses, squids, and cuttlefish, survived. Other shelled animals, the ammonites, that had also been so numerous during the Cretaceous, did not make it into the Tertiary. As the mammals came to rule the land during the Tertiary, so the bony fishes known to us today came to be masters of the seas.

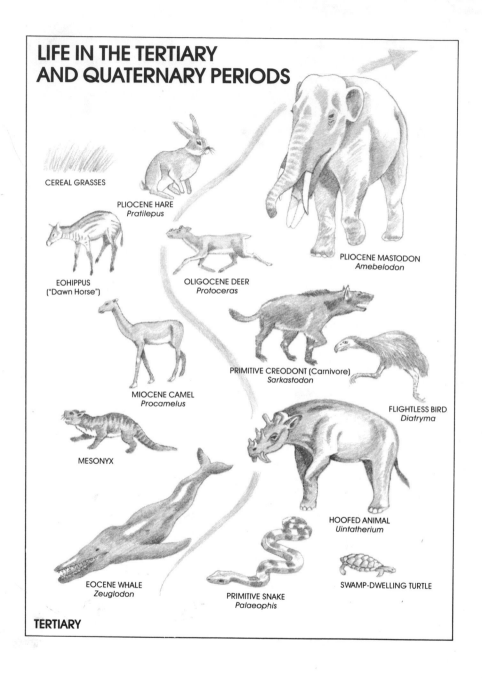

LIFE IN THE TERTIARY AND QUATERNARY PERIODS

CEREAL GRASSES

PLIOCENE HARE
Pratilepus

EOHIPPUS
("Dawn Horse")

OLIGOCENE DEER
Protoceras

PLIOCENE MASTODON
Amebelodon

MIOCENE CAMEL
Procamelus

PRIMITIVE CREODONT (Carnivore)
Sarkastodon

FLIGHTLESS BIRD
Diatryma

MESONYX

HOOFED ANIMAL
Uintatherium

EOCENE WHALE
Zeuglodon

PRIMITIVE SNAKE
Palaeophis

SWAMP-DWELLING TURTLE

TERTIARY

SABER-TOOTH CAT

GIANT BISON

GIANT BEAVER

MUSK OX

REINDEER

Australopithecus
(FORERUNNER OF MAN)

OAK TREE

PINE TREE

OCTOPUS

MODERN BIRD

ASPEN

MODERN HORSE
Equus

EARLY *Homo Sapiens*

QUATERNARY

A diorama of ocean life in the Tertiary period

MAMMALS RULE THE EARTH

The changing seasonal temperatures of the Tertiary most likely posed a challenge to land animals. The reptiles were cold-blooded and had no built-in way of warming themselves when the weather turned cold. They depended on the Sun for heat to keep them alive and active.

The newcomer mammals were different and had major advantages over the reptiles. They were warm-blooded; they could change their food into energy in the form of heat, enough heat to keep them warm during the chill of night or in regions gripped by seasonal cold. They also had coats of hair for warmth.

Unlike reptiles, which laid their eggs and depended on heat in the environment to hatch them, mammals kept their eggs warm inside their bodies. The eggs developed within the mother, who then gave birth to live offspring, who soon were able to care for themselves. Being warm-blooded was an important advantage.

Another advantage mammals had was a brain that became larger and kept improving in other ways during the Tertiary. We know this from fossil evidence. By comparison with the early mammals, the dinosaurs were not very "brainy." Compared with the size of their huge bodies, their brains were tiny. Even the earliest mammals had brains that were large compared with their body size. Intelligent activity, along with the advantage of being warm-blooded, assured the mammals of evolutionary success.

At the beginning of the Tertiary, according to fossil finds, there were about 15 major types of mammals. That was nearly twice as many as near the close of the Cretaceous. One of the newcomer species was to become the ancestor of modern horses. Ancestors of tapirs and rhinoceroses had also evolved by about this time. Early in the period bulky hoofed mammals about the size of a bear lived on plants in semitropical areas of western Colorado. Called *Barylambda*, they were an evolutionary dead end and so left no descendants.

By about 53 million years ago, in fact, there were a number of large and clumsy plant-eating mammals. One, known as *Uintatherium*, was a strange-looking beast with six horns on its head and face. It lived in present-day Wyoming.

There were also animals with sharp teeth for tearing and sharp claws. Ancestors of present-day flesh-eaters, these hunted the early hoofed mammals, which were an easy prey with their stumplike teeth more suited for grinding leaves and stems. By about 40 million years ago mammals about the size of a large dog had evolved and were ancestors of present-day deer, pigs, and camels.

Whales were common in the Tertiary seas, bats zigzagged through the air, and rabbits and rodents, including beavers, mice, and rats, were common. There also were many small insect-eating mammals. An important newcomer were small, tree-dwelling creatures that were to become ancestors of monkeys, apes, and humans.

By about 40 million years ago Greenland had broken away from Europe and no longer served as a bridge linking North America and Europe. Fossil evidence shows that up until that time the same kinds of animals had lived on both sides of the spreading Atlantic Ocean.

During the next 10 million years, many new types of mammals evolved. Certain other already existing types advanced, including cats and dogs. A number of other types became extinct. Among those that died out was a group known as the titanotheres. They included one awkward species as large as a small elephant and called *Brontotherium*. *Brontotherium* was a plant-eater that lived in the South Dakota–Nebraska region.

Most of the mammal groups that did so well during the Tertiary never managed to get to Australia because of that

Uintatherium, *a six-horned, plant-eating mammal of Tertiary times*

Whales, including Basilosaurus (shown here), were common in Tertiary seas.

Fossils of mollusks and other sea creatures found on what is now dry land. Fossil remains like these help scientists map the outline of ancient seas. Below: Giant kangaroos and wombats, marsupials of the early Cenozoic period.

continent's separation from the earlier Gondwana. Some primitive mammals of the Cretaceous did make it, however, and evolved along different lines. They evolved into a group of mammals called marsupials. Marsupials, including the kangaroo, carry their young in pouches. Since South America, Antarctica, and Australia were linked at the time the marsupials evolved, we also find marsupials in South America. They never made it to North America, since the two Americas were not linked at the time.

The marsupials evolved from mammalian ancestors that did make it from North America before the continents parted. Comparison of certain marsupial mammals with their North American nonmarsupial relatives proves the point. For example, the Australian Tasmanian wolf can be compared with the North American wolf; the Australian wombat with our ground hog; the rabbit-eared bandicoot with our rabbit; and the Australian mouse with our mouse.

Like Australian mammals, South American mammals also evolved apart from their North American ancestors. Examples are the sloth and armadillo. The land bridge that was to link North and South America was not formed until 3.5 million years ago, near the end of the Tertiary. At that time there was an exchange of mammalian groups between continents. In general, the North American mammals were more advanced, and when they migrated to South America they fared better than did the South American mammals who migrated to North America.

During the period between about 30 million and 5 million years ago North America and northern Europe were becoming cooler and drier. The earlier semitropical forests were crowded out. Grazing mammals did especially well during these times. There were many species of horses. In addition, there were giant pigs, camels, rhinoceroses, deer and antelopes, and mastodons. Bears, tigerlike cats, and several smaller meat-eaters evolved during this time. Among the

Mesonyx, *an early meat-eating mammal of the period*

smaller mammals were skunks, raccoons, weasels, and otters.

The years during this part of the Tertiary looked kindly on land life, and the mammals did especially well. The close of the period was another matter. Called by some the "autumn of the Cenozoic," because a harsh change in climate brought on the ice and cold, the end of this geologic period spelled doom to many species of plants and animals.

CHAPTER THREE

LIFE DURING THE QUATERNARY PERIOD

CHANGES ON THE LAND

The Quaternary period in Earth's geologic history began 1.8 million years ago. The late Tertiary had ushered in a new ice age, which lasted about 2.5 million years. The ice age saw the introduction of several giant mammals—the woolly mammoth, for instance. Humans also evolved during this period and marked the most recent tick of the Quaternary's geologic clock.

As we know from what is written in the rock and fossil records, ice ages have come and gone during Earth's geologic history. During the second half of the Quaternary alone, which spans the past 700,000 years, there have been at least seven separate ice ages, broken by warm periods called interglacials. We are living in an interglacial now.

There were many forced migrations of species as the great ice sheets ponderously ground their way overland during the ice ages. Sediments that were at times buried beneath the thick ice, and then exposed by melting during warm interglacial periods, give us a fossil record of the inhabitants who have come and gone. For instance, in central Europe we find fossil remains of woolly rhinoceroses, reindeer,

*The Northern mammoth, which flourished during
the ice age in the late Tertiary*

Arctic foxes, and mammoths—all cold-climate animals. Then, in sedimentary deposits of later times in the same area, we find fossil remains of elephants, deer, hippopotamuses, and hyenas—all warm-climate animals. By studying fossil pollen grains, plant scientists also have discovered valuable clues that help trace the times and locations of the Quaternary's ice sheets.

During the Quaternary ice ages much of Europe and Asia were covered with several thousand feet of ice. In North America, all of Canada and most of the United States as far south as the Ohio and Missouri rivers were covered with ice about 2 miles (3.2 km) deep. The Greenland and Antarctic ice caps today are reminders of how North America looked then.

CHANGES IN
PLANTS AND ANIMALS

The species of plants familiar to us today were already well established by the early Quaternary period. Although the coming of the ice affected vegetation throughout the deep-freeze periods of the Quaternary, it did not seem to kill off plant species in wholesale fashion, as was the case with animals. Instead, the ice acted as a great bulldozer that relocated plant species.

For example, in North America the hardwood forests of the north-central regions were destroyed by the ice. But as the advancing ice brought a cooler climate farther south, the hardwood forests simply reestablished themselves farther south, moving before the ice. Plants that had adapted to Arctic conditions, such as certain flowering plants and low shrubs, found new homes as the ice sheets displaced them from their cold lowland environment in the north to a similar environment, but one high on mountain slopes.

Such Arctic species today are plentiful on mountains that were in the paths of advancing glaciers. Certain plants growing today on the high slopes of the White Mountains of New Hampshire, and in Labrador, in earlier glacial times were lowland plants, but the lowland climate today is too warm for those plants to survive. Certain plants growing today near sea level around the rim of the Greenland icecap are found elsewhere only in the Himalayas and the Alps.

Pollen grains serve as important clues to past climates. Botanists (plant scientists) can trace the story of climate change in a certain area by studying the area's pollen grains. For example, suppose that a botanist digs a trench or makes a borehole at a certain location and then examines the layers of uncovered sediments, beginning at the bottom and working up toward the surface. If pollen grains of birch, spruce, and fir trees are found in the lower layer, the botanist knows that the climate at that time was cold and moist. That must be so, since those trees all do well in a cold, moist climate. If the sediments of the next higher layer on top of the first layer contain mostly pollen from oak and pine trees, that tells the scientist that the climate changed to a warm and dry one, since oak-pine forests do especially well in those conditions. If the third layer up contains pollen of alder and hemlock, that indicates that the climate next turned warm and moist, and so on up the ladder of sediments to the surface. So fossil pollen grains help us unravel the complex series of events in Earth's ever-changing climate.

Many major groups of animals of the early Quaternary evolved into giants that survived several invasions and retreats of ice but then mysteriously died out about 10,000 years ago. Among these was the mammoth. Mammoths were elephantlike animals that stood 13 feet (4 m) high at the shoulders and waved massive curving tusks just as long. They may have used their tusks as snowplows to uncover the grass on which they fed.

The Columbian mammoth, an elephantlike animal
with tusks that may have been used as snowplows

1. **Eohippus,** or "Dawn Horse," lived 50 million years ago. Only 10 to 20 inches (25 to 50 cm) high, it had toes instead of hoofs.

2. **Mesohippus** was about 24 inches (50 cm) tall. The side toes were smaller than the middle toe, and its trunk was longer and more slender than its ancestors'.

3. **Merychippus** (not pictured here) was up to 40 inches (100 cm) tall and was the first horse to graze. It had longer teeth than its predecessors.

5. **Equus,** the modern horse.

4. **Pliohippus** lived about 45 million years after the first Dawn Horse. The side toes had disappeared and the foot was a hoof. The size and features were about the same as today's horse.

THE EVOLUTION OF THE HORSE

THE EVOLUTION
OF HORSES

About 53 million years ago, near the beginning of the Tertiary period, we find fossil remains of an animal about the size of a small dog, called *Eohippus*, or "dawn horse." *Eohippus* was an unmistakable ancestor of modern horses. A forest-dweller, it had blunt teeth for grinding plants, four toes on each front foot, and three toes on each hind foot.

Then, some 37 million years ago, a newcomer appeared. Called *Mesohippus*, meaning "middle horse," it was about the size of a German shepherd dog, and all four feet had three toes, all the toes touching the ground. Like *Eohippus, Mesohippus* had teeth for grinding and fed on leaves and tender shoots. Wooded areas were its home.

About 25 million years ago another newcomer evolved. Called *Merychippus*, meaning "cud-chewing horse," it was about the size of a Great Dane dog. It had more powerful jaws and teeth that could grind up food that was tougher than leaves. Because grasses were widespread at the time of *Merychippus*, this new and larger horse left the forest and grazed on the plains.

From *Merychippus* there evolved several other kinds of horses. All became extinct except *Pliohippus*, which means "more of a horse." This animal evolved some 10 million years ago, was bigger than its ancestors, and, like the more recent ones, lived on the open plains, where it grazed. One major feature of *Pliohippus* was that it had one main toe on each foot, as do modern horses. The old side toes on *Pliohippus* by this time had shrunken to little more than short, thin strips.

Pliohippus was the ancestor of still other types, the sole survivor of which we know today as the modern horse group *Equus,* which includes donkeys, zebras, and onagers. *Equus* evolved about 2 million years ago in North America. Because Asia and Alaska were then joined by a land bridge due to the low level of the oceans at the time, *Equus* was able to migrate to Asia, and over the thousands of years that followed it spread the world over. When the North American ice age giant mammals died out between 14,000 and 6,000 years ago, *Equus* in America died out with them some 8,000 years ago. North America remained without horses until they were brought here from Europe by explorers about 500 years ago.

Horses and humans have a long history of living together. At first horses were a source of food, being killed when needed. Because they were easily tamed, they were later used to pull heavy loads, to carry riders, to pull a plow, and to carry weapons and warriors into battle. Like many other animals that humans have domesticated, horses probably would soon become extinct if humans decided that horses were no longer useful.

The giant mastodons, ancestors of today's elephants, also were awesome beasts that roamed the northeastern United States in great numbers. More than 100 mastodon skeletons have been found in New York State. The remains of mastodons, and of giant saber-toothed cats, have been found in the famous La Brea Tar Pits in Los Angeles, California. The giant beavers, as large as a black bear, could probably gnaw their way through a tree in minutes. And the bears of the period were larger than today's grizzly bears, the lions larger than today's lions.

Enormous ground sloths the size of elephants reared up on their hind legs to eat leaves and tender shoots two stories above the ground. In Africa there lived baboons bigger than gorillas, and pigs the size of rhinoceroses. South America also had its giants, among them rats the size of a calf and meat-eating birds that stood 8 feet (2.5 m) high. Then, between 14,000 and 6,000 years ago, all of the North American giants were gone.

What happened to all those wonderful beasts? One of the mysteries of the last ice age is why so many of them died out during the retreat of the ice. Gone, too, were the elephants, camels, horses, and dire wolves of earlier times.

Why such a great period of dying out? Some biologists feel that skilled hunters among the early American Indians of some 10,000 years ago killed off many of the giants, including the mammoth, longhorn bison, and horse. Archaeologists have come upon killing grounds, including some in Colorado, that contain the bones of hundreds of animals. Large groups of hunters apparently stampeded the animals and drove them into natural traps. The animals were then killed with stone-pointed spears and butchered.

Biologists also think that some species might have become extinct due to changes in climate. For example, mastodons were native to spruce forests. But the retreat of

Above: Neolithic hunters. Facing page: An artist's rendering of animal life in the La Brea Tar Pits

the ice was followed by a dry period, and many of the spruce forests were replaced by pine and hardwoods. Such a change in the environment may also have reduced the great beasts' numbers until there were too few left for a population to survive.

Fire also has been blamed, grass and forest fires started by lightning or set accidentally or on purpose by the early inhabitants of North America as they cleared the land for growing crops. Whatever the cause, or causes, all the "hugest, and fiercest, and strangest forms," as one biologist described them, disappeared almost overnight, geologically speaking.

Whenever this or that species dies out, it gives up a niche, a way of life it carves out in a certain part of the environment. That niche does not stay empty for long. It is quickly filled by a new species that evolves in the same place or by a foreign species that has wandered in from some distant corner of the world. Part of the story of evolution is competition for every available inch of living space, including the air, water, and land.

The last glacial period ended about 10,000 years ago. About 15,000 years ago, the Sun may have increased its energy output a little and so began a period of warming that quickened, or started, the melting of the great northern ice sheets. As the ice melted, patches of ground appeared, grasses and other plants were reestablished, and the land lifted somewhat as the great weight of the overlying ice became less. Meanwhile, the melting ice raised the level of the oceans, and the warming rays of the Sun heated them. This last part of the Quaternary also marked the beginning of rapid human growth, growth not only in numbers but in the development of a technology (tools) that enabled humans to advance and improve their lives in many important ways.

It is now time for us to ask where humans came from and to try to place ourselves in the overall pattern of evolution, for we surely are as much a part of that pattern as all of the other organisms whose evolution we have traced so far in this book.

CHAPTER FOUR

THE ARRIVAL
OF HUMANS

Where did humans come from? And when? Our search takes us back from 5 to 15 million years ago, to a time when gorillas, baboons, chimpanzees, orangutans, monkeys, and other modern primates had not yet evolved. Biologists define a primate as any mammal that has a complex brain, eyes located at the front of the head (which provide 3-D vision), 32 or 34 teeth, and hands with five fingers that can be used for grasping objects.

Because fossils tell us about the many kinds of animals that have lived in the past, and how they have changed with time, we begin our search for our human origins by studying the thousands of fossils of primates and their ancestors.

As we learned earlier, the first mammals were small, rat-like animals that evolved a little more than 65 million years ago, when the dinosaurs still ruled the land. In a relatively short time those mammal ancestors evolved into two different primate groups—the prosimians and the anthropoids. The prosimian branch includes today's tree shrews, lemurs, and tarsiers. The anthropoid branch includes monkeys, apes, and humans.

The oldest known primate fossil, dating to about the end of the Age of Reptiles, was discovered in Montana in 1965. By

*Facial features and skeletal structures as
they have evolved from fish to humans*

about 53 million years ago there were several different kinds of primates. All were small, about the size of a large squirrel or small cat. Some probably lived in trees and ate fruits and insects. However, by about 37 million years ago there were only a few primates left in North America, possibly as a result of a cooling and drying climate.

WHERE DID THE
EARLY PRIMATES GO?

Probably many primate species of North America migrated to South America, Africa, and Asia, where the climate was warmer. It is in Africa where we find the rapid evolution of primates into anthropoids. One reason may be that many new environments were created when crustal rock split open along a distance of 2,900 miles (4,600 km) and formed the East African Rift Valley. As a result, new desert, lake, tropical forest, open plain, swamp, and river environments were opened. As we learned in the last chapter, whenever a new environment is opened, there are individuals ready to occupy it.

Climbing the tree of evolution is like climbing a real tree. We start at the bottom, the trunk, and as we climb higher we must keep picking the branch that is most likely to get us to the top. Although some branches lead to dead ends, others keep on branching as we climb ever higher into the tree.

In our attempts to trace the origins of humans, the first branch we follow is the one marked "anthropoids," since it is the branch to which we belong. At this time in history the prosimians evolved in one direction and the anthropoids in a different direction.

What kind of animal started the anthropoid line? What did it look like?

The oldest known primate that many scientists think was a common ancestor of anthropoids was discovered in what is

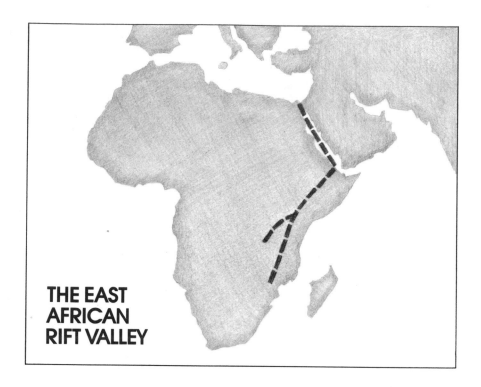

**THE EAST
AFRICAN
RIFT VALLEY**

now Egypt and lived some 30 million years ago. Called *Aegyptopithecus,* it was an apelike animal with a long tail and weighed about 12 pounds (6 kg). Scientists working in Burma in 1978 discovered the jawbones and teeth of a still older apelike ancestor of monkeys, apes, and humans. But there is no general agreement that these 40-million-year-old remains belong to a true anthropoid.

Higher up the anthropoid branch we find a more recent apelike animal, called *Dryopithecus,* which lived for about 15 million years, until about 10 million years ago. Fossil remains of this animal were first found by Louis Leakey in Kenya, Africa, in the 1930s. Since then many more fossils have been found

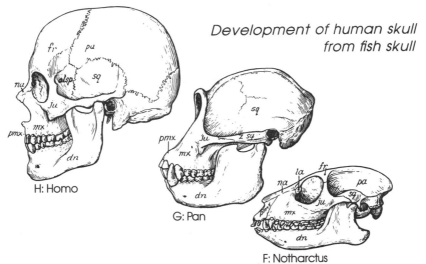

*Development of human skull
from fish skull*

H: Homo

G: Pan

F: Notharctus

E: Thrinaxodon

D: Seymouria

C: Eusthenopteron

H: MAN

G: APE

F: PRIMITIVE LEMUR

E: MAMMAL-LIKE REPTILE

D: PRIMITIVE TETRAPOD

C: LOBE-FIN FISH

B: JAW-BEARING FISH

A: OSTRACODERM

B: Acanthodes

A: Cephalaspis

far and wide—in China, Egypt, France, Germany, Greece, and Hungary, for example. Considering its long history, and the many habitats available, it is not surprising to find several offshoots of *Dryopithecus*. Some were as large as a gorilla, others the size of a gibbon. All probably spent most of their time as forest dwellers who ate fruit and leaves but once in a while may have ventured out onto the grasslands.

A BRANCH TO THE HUMAN LINE

In the 1960s, Leakey and his wife, Mary, again digging in Kenya, unearthed the upper jaw of a skull with teeth that were different from those of *Dryopithecus*. In some ways the teeth were like those of modern apes; in other ways they were like those of humans.

The skull was that of *Ramapithecus*, who lived in Africa, Asia, Greece, Turkey, and Hungary about 15 million years ago. Some scientists think *Ramapithecus* may mark the stage at which apes and humans parted ways. Although the evidence is slight, most agree that *Ramapithecus* should be grouped as an early member of the human branch, called hominids. But others regard *Ramapithecus* as an advanced ape.

The next landmark up the tree of evolution to modern humans is *Australopithecus*. They are our first known true hominid ancestors and may have lived as long ago as 5.5 million years, in the late Tertiary. The first such type was dis-

The Leakeys with bones they found in Kenya. The bones were judged to be about 2.6 million years old and probably belonged to Australopithecus.

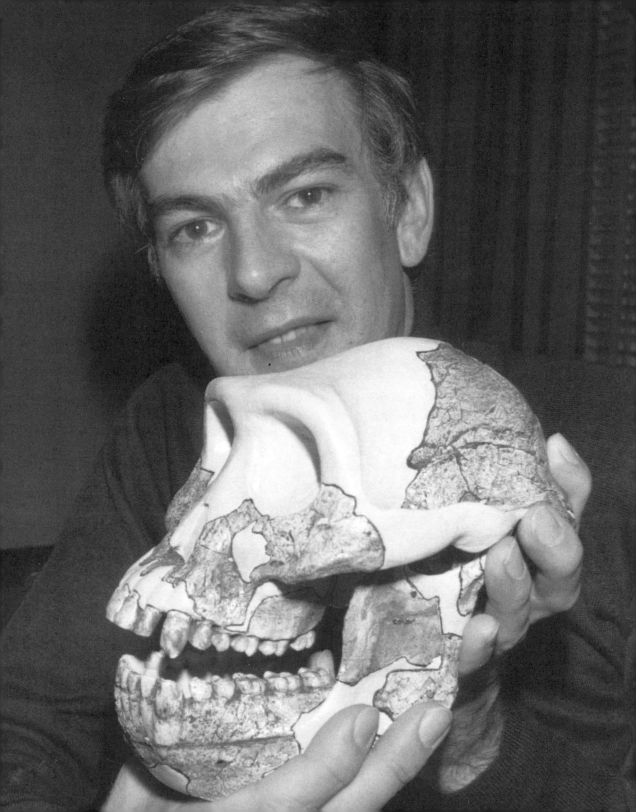

covered in 1924 in Taung, South Africa, by a scientist named Raymond Dart. It was the skull of a child about 6 years old with teeth that are human beyond question.

Other fossil finds—skulls, teeth, and bones—were made in both Africa and Java in the 1930s, and exciting new finds continue to be made almost every year. In 1974 a scientist named Donald C. Johanson uncovered in the Afar region of Ethiopia the most complete remains of *Australopithecus* yet found. The bones were those of a female, which Johanson named "Lucy," about 20 years old. Lucy had short legs, walked upright, and stood about 3 feet (1 m) tall. She is between 3.01 and 3.25 million years old.

MEET AN EARLY TRUE HUMAN

By about 700,000 years ago the offspring of another species of *Australopithecus* had spread to a number of new locations and climates, including areas gripped by the glacial ice that ushered in the Quaternary period. These people—they were in every way human, although not modern humans—took shelter in caves and learned the skill of building fire. They were also hunters. They were so like us that we place them in our group, called *Homo*. But because there are important differences between us and them, we give them a second name to suggest that difference—*Homo erectus*, meaning "upright man," as opposed to our group name of *Homo sapiens*, meaning "wise man."

These early people, who were well on their way to becoming modern humans, still had an apelike skull with powerful jaws and a large face with a low brow bone. But

*Donald Johanson with a
plaster cast skull of "Lucy"*

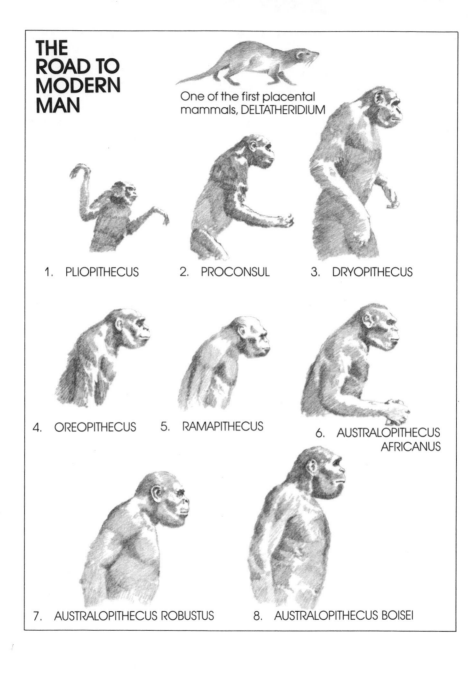

THE ROAD TO MODERN MAN

One of the first placental mammals, DELTATHERIDIUM

1. PLIOPITHECUS

2. PROCONSUL

3. DRYOPITHECUS

4. OREOPITHECUS

5. RAMAPITHECUS

6. AUSTRALOPITHECUS AFRICANUS

7. AUSTRALOPITHECUS ROBUSTUS

8. AUSTRALOPITHECUS BOISEI

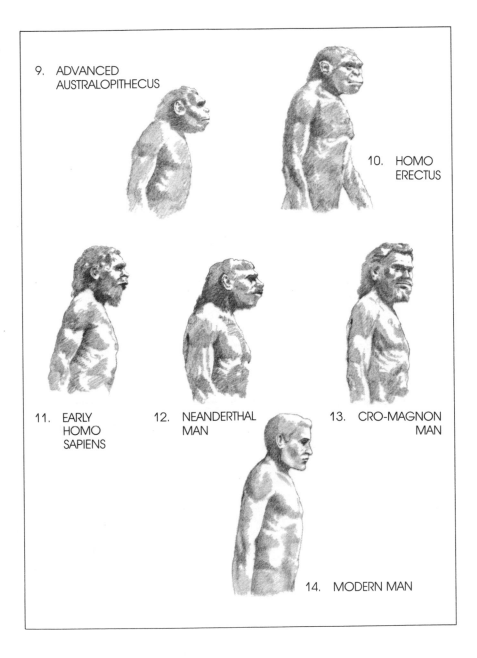

9. ADVANCED AUSTRALOPITHECUS

10. HOMO ERECTUS

11. EARLY HOMO SAPIENS

12. NEANDERTHAL MAN

13. CRO-MAGNON MAN

14. MODERN MAN

they were nearly our height. Their arms were a bit longer than ours and their legs a bit shorter. Their bodies were muscular and powerful; their walk was every bit as good as ours is. They also very likely had some speech, judging from their large brain. There were many of these early humans, and they lived until about 300,000 years ago. Their fossil remains have been found far and wide—in North Africa, Germany, Hungary, and China.

The first such fossil find, called Java Man, was made in 1891. One of the most valuable finds was made near Peking, China, in the 1920s by a scientist named Davidson Black. Black came upon a huge cave that had been the home of hunters for 70,000 years or so. Here he found the remains of cooking hearths, tools, food, and many bones of the hunters themselves. Many skulls found in the cave had been cracked open, suggesting that these cave dwellers had developed an appetite for human brains. The modern races of humans may have begun with offshoots of *Homo erectus*, those off-shoots being represented by Java Man, Peking Man, and Heidelberg Man of Germany.

ENTER *HOMO SAPIENS*

Some 300,000 years ago humans were living in Africa and Eurasia. They were little different from people living in those regions today. The major thing that would set them apart was their head shape—a slightly elongated head, a large face, a brow ridge, a slight chin, and powerful jaws. Over those 300,000 years to the present, evolution changed the head shape by making the large brow ridge smaller and adding a chin, among other things.

We know of a few *Homo sapiens* fossils dating back more than 200,000 years. For instance, two were found in France, one in England, and one in Germany. There were major dif-

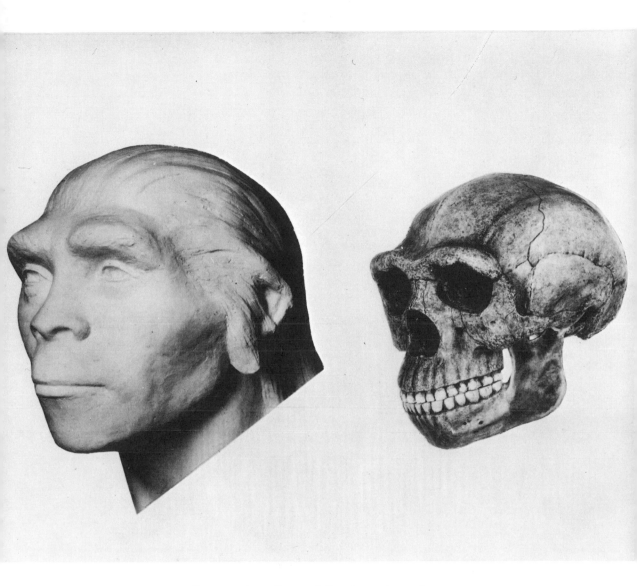

*Reconstruction of the head and
skull of a Peking woman*

ferences among these finds, mainly in head size, ruggedness of body, and jaw size.

The people living in northern Europe acquired a smaller jaw more quickly than the people living in southern France. The people living in England and Germany did not have large jaws, and their skulls were not very different from ours today.

Unhappily, we do not yet have a clear picture of how humans evolved over the last 100,000 years to the present. But every few years new evidence is unearthed that helps us fill in some of the gaps in our knowledge.

Until about 40,000 years ago there were many populations of large-jawed people known as Neanderthals. Neanderthals lived in many places—from Gibraltar across Europe into the Near East and central Asia. They lived in caves or in the open in tents made of animal skins. Their heads were slightly larger than ours, and they stood about 5 feet (1.5 m) tall and were powerfully built with large bones. They were around for about 60,000 years, but then suddenly and mysteriously died out.

OTHER POPULATIONS

About this time there were populations of humans other than Neanderthal. One group in the Middle East lived from about 100,000 to 30,000 years ago. Their fossils were discovered in caves in Palestine and in northern Iraq. Members of this group

A paleontologist chips away
at fossil bones in a rock matrix,
hoping to uncover valuable
clues concerning the history
of life on Earth.

contained both large-jawed individuals typical of Neanderthal and small-jawed individuals nearly like us.

Then, between 50,000 and 30,000 years ago, the large-jawed groups vanished and were replaced by a more modern people, known as Cro-Magnon. The earliest such groups came from South Africa (about 60,000 years ago), Southeast Asia (about 40,000 years ago), and Europe (30,000 years ago).

The mystery of the changeover from Neanderthal type to the modern type took place over a period of about 5,000 years. The only living descendants of the large-jawed people today are the Australian aborigines.

It now seems that Cro-Magnon populations entered North America at least 12,000 years ago, possibly earlier. They were from Siberia and likely settled their way southward, eventually populating South America all the way down to the southernmost tip.

Of the several hominid types that have come and gone over the past 15 million years or so, there remains today only one human species, *Homo sapiens*. Although we are of a single species, there are different races of us. Most biologists recognize only three races—Caucasoid (white-skinned), Negroid (black-skinned), and the intermediate Mongoloid type. There are five if Australian aborigines and American Indians are considered separate races.

As populations of other species have adapted to certain environments—the desert, grasslands, Arctic, freshwater, or ocean water—so have certain populations of our species become adapted to certain cubbyholes of the environment. For example, the Andean Indians live at high altitudes in the mountains of South America. Many people who climb to those heights of more than 16,000 feet (5,000 m) complain of "mountain sickness" due to the low air pressure, which makes it harder to breathe than at sea level. They become

Cro-Magnon cave painters

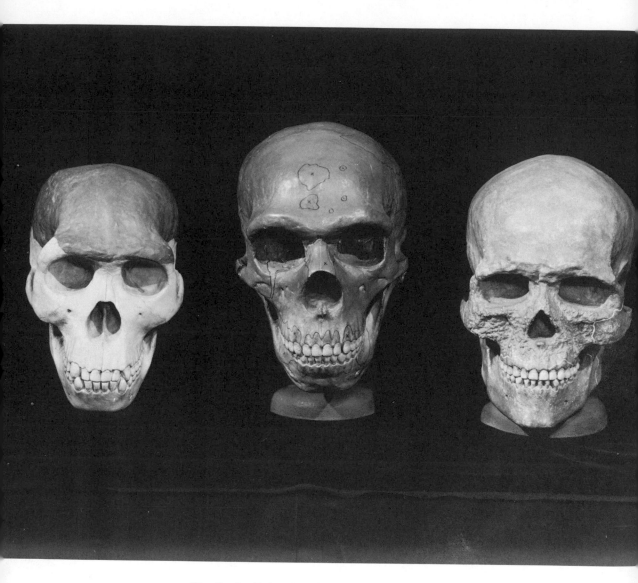

Skulls (left to right) of Pithecanthropus, Neanderthal, *and* Cro-Magnon man.

dizzy and sick to the stomach. Over the centuries the Andean Indians have adapted to high-altitude living by evolving a barrel-chested body with larger lungs and a larger supply of blood than people living at sea level have. Both features assure the body cells of getting a rich supply of oxygen—large lungs to take in a lot of air and a large supply of blood to carry oxygen to all the body cells.

Another example is the Eskimos, who have short fingers, which is an adaptation that in a cold climate saves valuable body heat that would be more quickly lost by long fingers. This is so because long fingers have a larger surface area from which more heat can escape.

Still another example is the dark skin of people native to tropical climates. Dark skin is an adaptation that protects the skin from damage by ultraviolet radiation from the Sun, which is more intense near the Equator than in the cloudy middle latitudes.

On the basis of the strong fossil evidence, it is hard to deny that human beings have evolved from earlier hominid groups. And it is just as hard to deny that those earlier hominids evolved from common ancestors that gave rise to both apes and hominids. But science still has much more to learn about the paths that human evolution have taken over the past 50 million years or so.

HUMAN POPULATION GROWTH

About 10,000 years ago, when people from Siberia may have first crossed over to North America, the total world population was only about 5 million. This is about five times the population of the state of Maine today, and only about one-fourth the population of Mexico City.

Most of the world's people then were food-gatherers—picking wild fruits, berries, and nuts, and killing what wild game they were able to. Life was uncertain, harsh, and short.

When people learned to plant seeds and tame certain animals as a source of food, life became easier. Food could be stored and used as needed. The shift from food-gathering to food-growing was a big change and meant that more people than ever before could be fed. By about the year 10 B.C. the world population had grown to between 200 and 300 million.

During the next 1,500 years the world population grew slowly. Famine and disease kept the population from growing rapidly. The leading killer diseases were tuberculosis, typhus, plague, and smallpox. Out of every 100 people, only four escaped smallpox. The disease killed one out of every four people. In the year 1720 plague killed 40,000 out of 90,000 people living in the French city of Marseilles. Plague may have killed between one-quarter and one-half of the entire population of Europe from time to time during the 1300s.

By the year 1650 the world population had grown to about 500 million. By 1850 it stood at about 1 billion. In 1970 the world population passed the 3.6 billion mark, adding from 70 to 75 million people to the planet each year. In mid-1985 the population reached 4.9 billion. By the year 2020 it will probably reach almost 8 billion.

The interesting thing about population growth is that the more people there are, the faster the population grows. For example, about the year 1800 it took 150 years for the world population to double. Today the doubling time is only about 40 years. In about 35 years from now, the doubling time may be only 15 years.

The question we must ask ourselves is, "What will happen if the world population just keeps growing out of control?" It couldn't just keep growing for many more years. There wouldn't be enough room left for all the people, and there

Plague killed one-quarter to one-half
the population of the ancient world.

HUMAN
POPULATION
GROWTH

8 BILLION

7 BILLION

6 BILLION

5 BILLION

4 BILLION

3 BILLION

2 BILLION

1 BILLION

1 MILLION

8000 BC

1650 AD 1850   1970 1985 2020

wouldn't be enough food to feed them all. The millions of starving people in Africa today are reminders of what could happen to most people on Earth if the population just keeps growing.

When we take even a brief look at the food problem, we can get some idea of the other problems that are also created by a runaway world population. To grow more food means using more fertilizers to grow crops and more pesticides to destroy insect pests that like to eat our crops.

More and more people also demand more automobiles, more clothes, more houses, more energy, and more everything else. To keep up with all of those needs means making still more of those fertilizers, pesticides, and producing the acid rain caused by more factories producing more and more goods. All of these things are polluting the environment, often at a risk to our health. Many of our lakes and rivers, and the fish that once lived in them, have already been destroyed. Smog makes cities like Los Angeles very unpleasant and unhealthy places to live in at times. Paper factories in places such as Rumford and Westbrook, Maine, regularly foul the air with chemicals that stink, and that thousands of people are forced to breathe in discomfort.

An increasing demand for energy causes a continuing increase in poisonous chemical and radioactive wastes that must be buried somewhere. It becomes more and more difficult to find "somewheres" to bury those wastes as people become educated about the dangers those wastes impose. A growing number of people put a greater and greater strain on the environment.

The problem of controlling widespread pollution is only part of the larger problem of controlling world population growth. To date, no one has come up with a workable way of halting world population growth. And that may well be one of the major problems in the evolution of *Homo sapiens* in the near future.

In the history of the evolution of living organisms on this planet, we have seen how changes in the environment have sometimes halted the evolution of certain animal or plant groups, at other times speeded it up. You may recall that the opening of several new environments caused by the splitting of the East African Rift Valley may have helped speed the evolution of primates into anthropoids. All of the species that followed, including the hominids, were at the mercy of their environment. And this has been so throughout geologic history. If they were not adapted to the environment in which they lived, they would die (or, if they had the intelligence, they could move to a more suitable environment).

Homo sapiens are different from all of their hominid ancestors. They are not mastered by the environment but master over it. If this or that aspect of the environment is unsatisfactory to us, we try to change it—by building dams to control river flow, converting deserts into farmland, and controlling through medicines and technology the many diseases that once spelled death for millions.

With these powers to improve our health and alter the environment to suit our needs, we may have slowed or in some other way changed the way our species will evolve in the future. Perhaps we will even prove to be intelligent enough, as a species, to control our world population growth and live in harmony with the splendid offerings of Earth.

Increased pollution is one
result of overpopulation.

CREATIONISM AND EVOLUTION

Does everyone accept evolution as a fact?

Almost all biologists and other scientists are convinced by the fossil record that evolution has taken place in the past and that it continues today. All life forms known to us today and in the past, they say, gradually evolved from earlier and simpler life forms; and those earlier and simpler life forms in turn evolved from natural substances such as amino acids and proteins that formed at the beginning of Earth's history as a planet. Most scientists also trust the many ways they have of dating the age of Earth's rocks and fossils. The evidence shows that Earth has a very long geological history, one that goes back some 4.6 billion years.

But there are many people—some scientists among them—who deny that evolution has taken place in the past or that it is taking place now. Most of the people who say no to evolution do so on religious grounds. They say the Bible should be believed word for word, that everything written in the Bible is true exactly the way it is described. They believe that because they further believe that the Bible is the "word of God." For example, in the Bible's Book of Genesis there are two chapters that say that God created the world and all life in six days. Belief in that Biblical description of the creation of the world is called creationism. The creationists therefore deny evolution because they see it as an attack on the Bible.

The creationists believe that the world is only about 10,000 years old, not 4.6 billion years old. They say that the scientific methods of telling the age of rocks and fossils cannot be trusted. According to them, humans and dinosaurs lived side by side and the last dinosaurs died out only a few thousand years ago, about the time the first American Indians crossed over to North America from Siberia. This has to mean that the dinosaurs lived during an ice age. Recall that the dinosaurs were reptiles, cold-blooded animals. There is no scientifically proven way a cold-blooded dinosaur could have lived in the cold climate of a North American ice age. The creationists further believe that the scientific views about the origin of the Solar System are wrong, and that their "research" will prove that what the Bible says about the origin of the world and life is true in every detail.

The creationists also deny that the fossil record shows patterns of gradual changes in plants and animals from one geologic period to the next. They say that God created all plants and animals exactly as we know them today.

Not all religious people agree with the creationists. Many look on the Bible as a source of spiritual enlightenment and do not insist on its word-for-word accuracy, as if it were a textbook of science. Unlike the creationists, they have no problem teaching evolution in their classrooms.

Religion and science have two different ways of understanding the world. Religion is based on faith and belief in one or more supernatural beings—one god or many gods—who cause all things to happen. In religion, God is the final authority.

Science does not accept authority. Scientists try to explain natural events by making observations of what they can measure—a fossil or a force, such as the skull of a dinosaur or gravity, for instance. An explanation based on those observations then becomes a scientific theory. The more testing the theory can stand up against, the more reliable the theory becomes. Today there is an overwhelming collection of evidence showing that evolution is a fact. However, there still are several theories about *how* evolution works. It is those theories, not evolution itself, that are subject to change in the face of new discoveries.

While the truths of science are always subject to change, that is not so of religion. The truths of religion are unchanging and eternal. That is a very important difference between science and religion. One of the things that makes religion so appealing is the comfort it provides through its never-changing truths that ultimately come from God. One of the things that makes science such an appealing and exciting quest for knowledge is that its truths are always subject to change based on the uncovering of new evidence. Religion does not need evidence to support what the Bible says. In science, today's truths often run the risk of becoming tomorrow's myths.

GLOSSARY

Adaptation. The process whereby a plant or animal population adjusts, through the fitness of certain of its individual members, to changes in the environment—a change in climate, for example. Sometimes the environmental changes are so severe that no individuals in the population are able to survive, and the population dies out. In other cases, certain individuals are "fitter" than most others and are able to survive. They may pass on their fitness to their offspring and so build up the population again.

Anthropoid. Those higher primates including apes, monkeys, and humans.

Cenozoic era. The geologic time period that began about 65 million years ago and is divided into two periods—the Tertiary and Quaternary. It also is called the Age of Mammals.

Cold-blooded. Cold-blooded animals, such as reptiles, have a body temperature that changes with the temperature of the environment. Warm-blooded animals, such as mammals, maintain a constant body temperature and so enjoy a survival advantage over cold-blooded species.

Cro-Magnon. Early *Homo sapiens* who were more modern than and replaced the Neanderthals about 30,000 years

TIME SCALE OF EARTH HISTORY

Time Scale	ERAS	Duration of Periods	PERIODS		DOMINANT ANIMAL LIFE
10 20 40 60	CENOZOIC 70 MILLION YEARS DURATION		Quaternary	Recent Pleistocene	Man
		70	Tertiary	Pliocene Miocene Oligocene Eocene Paleocene (EPOCHS)	Mammals
80 100	MESOZOIC 120 MILLION YEARS DURATION	50	Cretaceous		
150		35	Jurassic		
		35	Triassic		Dinosaurs
200	PALEOZOIC 350 MILLION YEARS DURATION	25	Permian		Primitive reptiles
		20	Pennsylvanian		
250		30	Mississippian		
300		65	Devonian		Amphibians
350		35	Silurian		Fishes
400		75	Ordovician		Invertebrates
450 500		90	Cambrian		
PROTEROZOIC ARCHAEOZOIC (Figures in millions of years)		(Figures in millions of years)	1500 million years duration		Beginnings of life

Only during the last 500,000,000 years have plants and animals produced hard parts capable of being fossilized. Here is a simplified chart of that quarter of the earth's history.

Another visual representation of the eras in Earth's history

ago. The earliest Cro-Magnon groups came from South Africa about 60,000 years ago. Cro-Magnon populations were in North America at least 12,000 years ago, possibly much earlier, having crossed over a bridge of land once linking Siberia to Alaska.

Erosion. The destructive effects of water, heat, frost, wind, ice, and acid rain, which mechanically or chemically break down solid rock into loose particles, or sediments.

Evolution. The process that explains the various patterns of biological change that ultimately causes the success (adaptation) or failure (extinction) of species and produces new species of plants and animals. As it has in the past, biological evolution continues to take place today. Charles Darwin and Alfred Russell Wallace are credited with developing the basic principles of evolution.

Extinction. The total disappearance of an entire species. Once a species has become extinct, it is gone forever.

Fault. A crack or break in Earth's crustal rock. Two surfaces along a fault may strain against each other until the pressure is so great that the two surfaces slip, or snap. The snapping action causes an earthquake. The San Andreas Fault in California is the dividing line between two great blocks of Earth's crust pressing against each other and the cause of many earthquakes.

Fossils. The remains of once-living plants or animals. Fossils may be bits of bone or teeth or even a footprint or other imprint left from long ago. Most fossils are found in sedimentary rock and are usually more than 10,000 years old.

Geosyncline. A great trench that forms in Earth's crust. Over many years, sediments flowing into the geosyncline depress the trench into the crust. Pressure from the sides of the trench squeezes the sediments down and at the same time thrusts them up. Some mountains are formed this way.

Habitat. The environment, along with all the organisms, in which a species lives.

Hominids. Any primate in the human family. Modern humans are the only surviving members. A group known as *Australopithecus* may have been the first true hominids and lived as long ago as 5.5 million years, in the late Tertiary.

Homo erectus. A group of hominids that were clearly human but not yet modern humans. *Homo erectus* hunted, lived in caves, and knew the art of starting fire. The name means "upright man."

Homo sapiens. The group name of modern humans. It means "wise man."

Ice age. A span of thousands of years during which glaciers several thousand feet thick advance over the land and cause a cooling climate. Because so much water is locked up as ice during a glacial period, sea level drops.

Interglacial. A period of warming between two ice ages. We are probably living during an interglacial now.

Invertebrate. Any group of animals lacking a backbone. The earliest life forms on Earth were invertebrates who lived in water.

Mammal. Any vertebrate animal that has warm blood, a covering of hair, gives birth to its young (with two exceptions), and suckles its young.

Mesozoic era. The "time of middle life," spanning some 160 million years and usually broken down into three periods—the Triassic, Jurassic, and Cretaceous. The Mesozoic era was the era that directly preceded the Cenozoic. It ended with a mass extinction that wiped out the dinosaurs and saw the rise of mammals.

Mid-Atlantic Ridge. A great crack in Earth's crust between North America and Europe, and between South America and Africa. As this crack continues to widen, the Atlantic

Ocean grows wider and Europe and North America drift farther apart, at the rate of about an inch a year.

Neanderthal Man. One of a group of large-jawed humans who lived in many places around the world for about 60,000 years, but then suddenly and mysteriously died out. Neanderthals lived in caves or tents made of animal skins; they buried their dead and had a limited language.

Niche. All aspects of the environment, and a species' interaction with that environment, that influence the well being of the species.

Pangaea. The supercontinent that existed about 220 million years ago when all the continents were merged into one. By about 135 million years ago, Pangaea had broken up and drifted apart into a northern half called Laurasia and a southern half called Gondwana.

Primate. Any mammal that includes anthropoids and prosimians, the two major groups into which primates split more than 50 million years ago. The anthropoids became the ancestors of the first hominids.

Prosimian. (meaning "before ape") Any member of the lower order of primates that includes lemurs, lorises, tarsiers, and bush babies, as well as many fossil forms.

Quaternary period. The second of the two periods of the Cenozoic era. The Quaternary period began 1.8 million years ago and brings us up to modern times.

Rift valley. A trench through which molten rock from the mantle wells up and flows out onto the surrounding crustal rock; for example, the Mid-Atlantic Ridge runs several thousand miles north and south along the floor of the mid-Atlantic Ocean, causing seafloor spreading.

San Andreas Fault. A great crack in the rock crust. Formed about 25 million years ago, the fault runs north and south a few miles inland along most of California's coast. From time to time movements of crustal rock cause the two faces of the fault to rub against each other and snap, producing earthquakes. The San Andreas Fault is the dividing line between two great blocks of Earth's crust.

Sediments. The loose bits and pieces of clay, mud, sand, gravel, lime, and other earth materials that pile up century after century and become squeezed by the great weight of new sediments above. Eventually, such sediment heaps may be thrust up as new mountains.

Species. Any one kind of animal or plant group, each member of which is like every other member in certain important ways. All populations of such a group must be capable of interbreeding and producing healthy offspring.

Tertiary period. The first of the two periods of the Cenozoic era. The Tertiary spanned some 63 million years, beginning 65 million years ago and ending 1.8 million years ago.

Vertebrate. Any group of animals having a backbone, which provides support and protects the nerves of the spinal cord.

Warm-blooded. Warm-blooded animals have self-regulating temperatures, which means that they generate their own heat rather than depend on heat from the air or land, as cold-blooded animals (for example, reptiles) do.

INDEX

ABOUT THE AUTHOR

Roy Gallant is a professor of English at the University of Southern Maine and director of the university's Southworth Planetarium. He is a former editor in chief of the Natural History Press of The American Museum of Natural History in New York City, and former managing editor of *Scholastic Teacher.* Among his other activities, he is currently serving as an earth science consultant for *Science and Children,* published by the National Science Teachers Association.

In addition, Professor Gallant is author of more than fifty science text and trade books for young readers and adults.